C000216522

This edition published by Ravette Publishing 2007.

Printed and bound in Belgium

ISBN 13: 978-1-84161-275-1

RAVETTE PUBLISHING

Lead me

not into

temptation

If in doubt, add more wine

I have a drinking problem, two hands

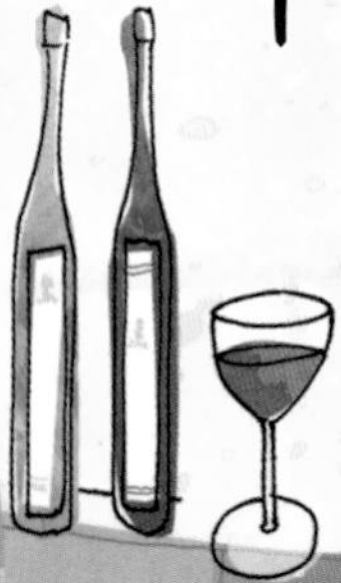

I'm on an
alcohol
diet,

so far I've lost

two

days

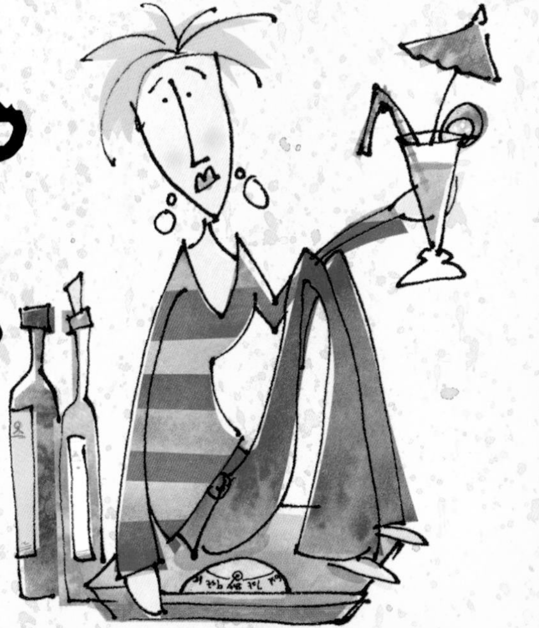

The years have been kind, it's the weekends that have done the damage

...waking
up does

I don't know,
I don't care,
that's why they
put me in
charge

I take life with
a pinch of salt,
a wedge of lime
and a shot
of tequila

Seen it all,
done it all,
can't remember
most of it

The face is familiar but I can't quite

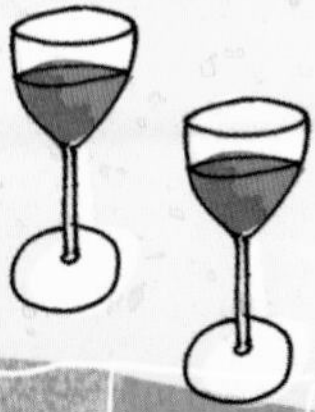

remember
my name!

One Tequila,
two Tequila,
three Tequila,
floor!

I love to cook with wine, sometimes I even put it in the food

The whole world is about three drinks behind

I can only please
one person per day.
Today is not
your day.

I read about
the evils
of drinking
wine

I can see clearly now the brain has gone

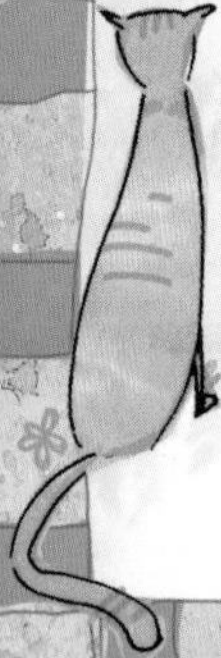

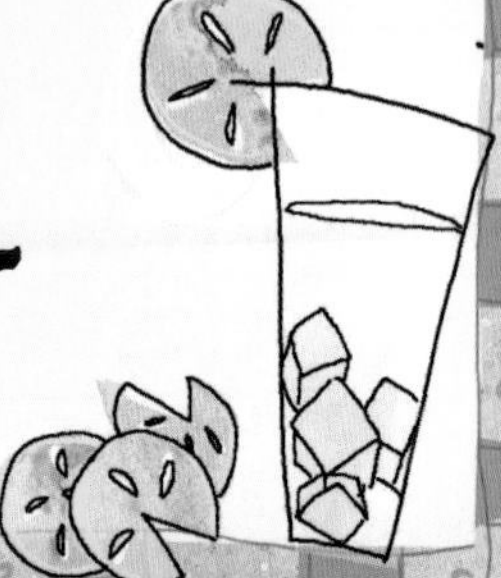

Christmas is a time for good will, not good will power

Other BORN TO SHOP titles available ...

	ISBN	Price
All men are created equal... equally useless	978-1-84161-257-7	£4.99
Another day in paradise	978-1-84161-255-3	£4.99
Born to Shop non stop (Aug 07)	978-1-84161-283-6	£4.99
100% gorgeous (Aug 07)	978-1-84161-284-3	£4.99
I never met a calorie I didn't like	978-1-84161-256-0	£4.99
Friends are the family we choose for ourselves	978-1-84161-254-6	£4.99
'M' is for Mother, not for Maid	978-1-84161-274-4	£4.99

HOW TO ORDER   Please send a cheque/postal order in £ sterling, made payable
to 'Ravette Publishing' for the cover price of the books and
allow the following for post & packaging ...

UK & BFPO	70p for the first book & 40p per book thereafter
Europe & Eire	£1.30 for the first book & 70p per book thereafter
Rest of the world	£2.20 for the first book & £1.10 per book thereafter

RAVETTE PUBLISHING LTD
Unit 3 Tristar Centre, Star Road, Partridge Green, West Sussex RH13 8RA
Tel: 01403 711443   Fax: 01403 711554   Email: ravettepub@aol.com

Prices and availability are subject to change without prior notice.